Mediterranean Refresh Cookbook for Beginners

Mediterranean healthy diet recipes to cook quick and easy meals

Copyright©2022

Contents

Contents

Introduction

The Mediterranean diet is both delicious and nutritious, thanks to its abundance of savory components such as fruits, vegetables, whole grains, and heart-healthy fats.

It's also linked to a slew of health benefits, including supporting brain function, promoting heart health, and regulating blood sugar levels, among others.

Although there are no hard and fast rules for following the Mediterranean diet, there are a number of general guidelines you can follow to incorporate the diet's principles into your daily routine

This book delves deeper into the Mediterranean diet, including what it is, how to follow it, and how it can benefit your health including amazing recipes which you can try with ease.

Mediterranean diet

The Mediterranean diet is based on the traditional cuisine that people in Mediterranean nations like France, Spain, Greece, and Italy used to eat.

The patients in this study were extremely healthy and had a low chance of developing a variety of chronic diseases, according to the researchers.

Although there are no particular dietary guidelines, fruits, vegetables, whole grains, legumes, nuts, seeds, and heart-healthy fats are often encouraged. Refined cereals, processed meals, and added sugar should all be avoided.

A growing body of evidence suggests that the Mediterranean diet can help people lose weight and prevent heart attacks, strokes, type 2 diabetes, and premature death.

As a result, the Mediterranean diet is frequently suggested to people who want to enhance their health and protect themselves from chronic disease.

Advantages that could be gained

A extensive number of health benefits have been connected to the Mediterranean diet.

It is good for your heart.

The Mediterranean diet's capacity to boost heart health has been thoroughly researched.

Studies have linked the Mediterranean diet to a reduced risk of heart disease and stroke.

One study compared the Mediterranean diet to a low-fat diet and found that the Mediterranean diet was more successful at slowing plaque buildup in the arteries, which is a key risk factor for heart disease

.

Benefits of the Mediterranean diet

The Mediterranean diet can help lower diastolic and systolic blood pressure, which is good for heart health.

Helps to maintain a healthy blood sugar level

The Mediterranean diet encourages a variety of nutrient-dense foods, including fruits, vegetables, nuts, seeds, whole grains, and heart-healthy fats.

As a result, adhering to this eating pattern may aid in the stabilization of blood sugar levels and the prevention of type 2 diabetes.

Multiple studies have discovered that following a Mediterranean diet can lower fasting blood sugar levels and enhance hemoglobin A1C levels, a test used to assess long-term blood sugar control.

Insulin resistance, a disorder in which the body's capacity to use insulin to efficiently manage blood sugar levels is impaired, has also been linked to the Mediterranean diet.

It helps to keep the brain healthy.

Several studies suggest that the Mediterranean diet is good for your brain and may even prevent you from cognitive loss as you age.

Other research has discovered that the Mediterranean diet may be linked to a reduced risk of dementia, cognitive impairment, and Alzheimer's disease.

Furthermore, one major review found that eating a Mediterranean diet improved cognitive function, memory, attention, and processing speed in healthy older persons.

The best way to follow the Mediterranean diet

Potatoes, Vegetables, fruits, whole grains, nuts, seeds, extra virgin olive oil, legumes, herbs, spices, fish, and seafood are all healthy foods to consume.

Yogurt, Poultry, eggs, cheese should be consumed in moderation.

Red meat, sugar-sweetened beverages, added sugars, processed meat, refined grains, refined oils, and other highly processed foods should be consumed only in moderation.

Foods to consume

Salmon, sardines, trout, mackerel, shrimp, oysters, clams, crab, tuna, and mussels are examples of fish and seafood.

Turkey, Chicken, and duck are examples of poultry.

Chicken, quail, and duck eggs are available.

Cheese, yogurt, and milk are examples of dairy products.

Garlic, basil, sage, mint, rosemary, nutmeg, cinnamon, and pepper are some of the herbs and spices used.

Olive oil, avocados, and extra virgin olive oil are all good sources of healthy fats.

Foods to avoid

When following the Mediterranean diet, you should avoid the following processed foods and ingredients:

Added sugar can be found in a variety of meals, but it is particularly prevalent in ice cream, soda, sweets, table sugar, syrup, and baked goods.

Crackers, White bread, pasta, tortillas, and chips are examples of refined grains.

Margarine, fried meals, and other processed foods contain trans fats.

Cottonseed oil, Soybean oil, canola oil, and grapeseed oil are examples of refined oils.

Meat that has been processed, such as beef jerky fast food, sausages, hot dogs, deli meats, microwave popcorn, and granola bars are examples of highly processed foods.

Beverages

On a Mediterranean diet, water should be your primary beverage.

This diet also includes a small amount of red wine each day — perhaps one glass.

This is, however, entirely voluntary, and wine should be avoided.

This is, however, entirely optional, and wine should be avoided by certain people, such as those who are pregnant, have trouble drinking in moderation, or are taking certain drugs that may interact with alcohol.

On the Mediterranean diet, coffee and tea are also healthful beverage options. Be wary of using a lot of extra sugar or cream.

Sugar-sweetened beverages, such as soda or sweet tea, are rich in added sugar and should be avoided. Fruit juice is acceptable in moderation, but you're better off eating entire fruits to obtain the fiber benefit.

Nutritious snacks

If you get hungry in between meals, there are lots of healthy snack options available on the Mediterranean diet.

Here are some suggestions to get you started:

a fruit piece, baby carrots, mixed berries, and grapes Yogurt from Greece salt and pepper hard-boiled egg sliced bell peppers with guacamole apple slices with almond butter fresh fruit and cottage cheese

Going out to eat

Many restaurant menu items are Mediterranean-friendly. Choose whole grains, veggies, legumes, fish, and healthy fats wherever possible. It's also important to eat and relish your dinner with nice company, so pick something that sounds delicious.

Tips to the Mediterranean diet

Here are a few pointers to help you adapt foods when dining out:

As a main course, opt for fish or seafood.

Inquire with your server if your meal may be prepared using extra virgin olive oil.

Instead of butter, use olive oil on whole-grain toast. Vegetables can be added to your order.

Recipes

Greek salad with grilled chicken and quinoa

Ingredients

Ingredients

- 1 deseeded and finely chopped red chili

- 1 red onion, finely sliced

- 1 smashed garlic clove

- 100g feta cheese, crumbled

- small bunch mint leaves, chopped juice, and zest ½ lemon

- 25g butter 225g quinoa

- 300g vine tomato, roughly diced, and a handful of pitted black Kalamata olives

- 400g tiny chicken fillets

- Extra-virgin olive oil, 112 tablespoon

Method

Cook the quinoa according to the package directions, then rinse and drain completely.

In the meantime, make a paste using butter, chili, and garlic. Season the chicken fillets with 2 teaspoons olive oil and a pinch of salt and pepper.

Cook for 3-4 minutes on each side in a hot griddle pan or until cooked through. Place on a platter and top with the spicy butter before setting aside to melt.

Toss the tomatoes, olives, onion, feta, and mint together in a mixing basin. Toss in the quinoa that has been cooked. Season to taste with the remaining olive oil, lemon juice, and zest. Serve with the chicken fillets on top and any buttery chicken juices poured on top.

Mediterranean potato salad

Ingredients

- 1 garlic clove, crushed
- 1 small onion, thinly sliced
- 1 tablespoon olive oil
- 1 teaspoon oregano, fresh or dried
- 100g roasted red pepper, from a jar, sliced
- 25g black olive
- 300g new potato, halved if large

- 400g can cherry tomatoes
- sliced handful basil leaves, torn

Method

In a saucepan, heat the oil, then add the onion and simmer for 5-10 minutes, or until tender.

Cook for 1 minute after adding the garlic and oregano. Add the tomatoes and peppers, season well, and cook for 10 minutes on low heat.

In the meantime, boil the potatoes in salted water for 10-15 minutes, or until soft. Drain well, combine with the sauce, and serve hot with olives and basil on top.

Crispy fried calamari & aïoli

Ingredients

- 500g squid, tubes and tentacles, cleaned vegetable oil, for deep-frying
- 50g cornflour
- ¼ teaspoon baking
- 50g plain flour

For the aïoli

- ½ lemon, juiced
- 1 large garlic clove, finely grated pinch of saffron
- 150g mayonnaise

Method

Squid tentacles should be cut off and placed in a bowl. Add the squid tubes to the bowl, into 1cm thick rings. In a big heavy-bottomed pan, heat the oil over low heat, filling it no more than two-thirds full.

In a small bowl, combine the mayonnaise, garlic, saffron, and lemon juice for the aoli.

Combine the squid, flour, cornflour, baking powder, cayenne, and 12 teaspoon salt in a mixing bowl.

Deep-fry the squid in batches for 2 minutes, or until lightly golden and crisp, or until a cube of bread is dropped in and turns golden brown in 30 seconds, according to a thermometer. Place on a tray coated with kitchen paper and set aside. Serve the food.

Courgette & quinoa-stuffed peppers

Ingredients

- 250g packs ready-to-eat quinoa
- 4 red peppers
- 85g feta cheese, finely crumbled handful parsley
- courgette quartered lengthways, and thinly sliced

Method

Preheat the oven to 200 degrees Fahrenheit. Remove the seeds from each pepper by cutting them in half through the stalk.

Place the peppers cut-side up on a baking sheet, drizzle with 1 tablespoon olive oil, and season with salt and pepper. 15 minutes of roasting

In a small frying pan, heat 1 teaspoon olive oil, then add the courgette and cook until tender. Remove the pan from the heat and add the quinoa, feta, and parsley. Season with salt and pepper.

Divide the quinoa mixture between the pepper halves and return to the oven to heat through for 5 minutes. If desired, serve with a green salad.

Bacon & brie omelet wedges with summer salad

Ingredients

- 1 cucumber, halved, deseeded, and sliced on the diagonal
- 1 teaspoon Dijon mustard
- 1 teaspoon red wine vinegar
- 100g brie, sliced
- 2 tablespoon olive oil
- 200g radishes, quartered
- 200g smoked lardons
- 6 eggs, lightly beaten
- small bunch chives snipped

Method

Preheat the grill and a small pan with 1 teaspoon of oil. Fry the lardons until they are crisp and brown. Drain on paper towels.

In a nonstick frying pan, heat 2 teaspoons of oil. Combine the eggs, lardons, chives, and black pepper in a mixing bowl. Pour into the frying pan and cook over low heat until the mixture is semi-set, then top with the brie. Grill till golden and set. Just before serving, remove from the pan and cut into wedges.

In a separate bowl, combine the remaining olive oil, vinegar, mustard, and spices. Toss the cucumber and radishes in with the omelet wedges and serve.

Herbed lamb cutlets with roasted vegetables

Ingredients

- 1 red onion, cut into wedges
- 1 tablespoon olive oil
- 2 peppers, any color
- 8 lean lamb cutlets
- courgettes, sliced into chunks
- 2 large sweet potatoes, peeled and cut into chunky pieces
- 1 tablespoon mint leaves, chopped

- 2 tablespoon thyme leaf, chopped

Method

Preheat the oven to 220 degrees Celsius. Drizzle the oil over the peppers, sweet potato, courgettes, and onion in a large baking dish. Season with a generous amount of freshly ground black pepper. Preheat oven to 350°F and roast for 25 minutes.

In the meantime, cut the fat from the lamb as much as possible. Pat the herbs all over the lamb with a few twists of ground black pepper.

Remove the vegetables from the oven, turn them over, and push them to one side of the baking sheet. Return the cutlets to the oven for 10 minutes after placing them on the heated tray.

Cook for a further 10 minutes, or until the veggies and lamb are soft and faintly browned. On the stove, combine everything.

Chorizo pilaf

Ingredients

- 1 large onion, thinly sliced

- 1 tablespoon olive oil

- 1 teaspoon smoked paprika

- 250g baby cooking chorizo, sliced

- 250g basmati rice

- 4 garlic cloves, crushed

- 400g can chopped tomato

- 600ml stock

- fresh bay leaves

- lemon, zest peeled off in thick strips, plus wedges to serve

- small bunch parsley, chopped

Method

In a large lidded pan, heat the oil. Cook for 5 minutes, or until the onion is tender and brown. Add the chorizo and push it to the edge of the pan. Cook, stirring occasionally until gently browned and some of the oils have leaked into the pan.

Toss in the garlic, paprika, and tomatoes. After 5 minutes of bubbling over medium heat, add the rice, stock, lemon zest, and bay leaves. Bring everything to a boil, stirring constantly. Cook for 12 minutes with the cover on over very low heat.

Remove the pan from the heat and set it aside to steam for 10-15 minutes. Serve with lemon wedges for squeezing over the top after stirring in the parsley.

Broad bean & feta cheese toasts

Ingredients

- 1 tablespoon extra-virgin olive oil
- 1 teaspoon lemon juice
- 10 cherry tomatoes, halved
- 100g feta cheese
- 2 tablespoon chopped or shredded mint leaves
- 350g broad bean, fresh or frozen
- 4 thin slices of baguettes
- 50g bag mixed salad leaf

Method

Boil a small amount of water in a small saucepan. Return the pot to a boil and cook the beans for another 4 minutes. Drain in a colander under cold running water. In a basin, press each bean out of its skin.

Scatter the mint leaves over the crumbled feta. 2 teaspoon oil, a healthy grind of black pepper, and a drizzle of the oil Toss everything together.

Toss with the remaining olive oil and lemon juice the salad leaves and tomatoes. Divide the mixture between two plates. Toast the bread on both sides under the grill or in a toaster until golden and crisp.

To serve, spread the bean and cheese mixture onto the heated toasts and serve with the salad on the side.

Caponata

Ingredients

For the caponata

- 1 garlic clove

- 100ml olive oil

- 2 long shallots, chopped

- 2 teaspoon caper, soaked if salted

- 3 large aubergines, cut into 2cm cubes

- 4 celery sticks, sliced

- 50ml red wine vinegar

- 4 large plum tomatoes, chopped

- 50g raisin

- handful toasted pine nuts and basil leaves

Method

Pour the olive oil into a big heavy-bottomed skillet or casserole, then add the aubergines and cook over medium heat. Cook for 20 minutes, or until they're tender. Scoop the aubergines out of the pan, leaving some olive oil behind.

Cook for about 5 minutes, or until the shallots are tender and transparent. Cook the tomatoes slowly until they break down and become a soft mush, then return the aubergines to the pan.

Add the celery, vinegar, capers, raisins, season with salt and pepper, and cover with a lid. Cook for 35 minutes on low heat, or until all the vegetables are tender. Stir slowly so the stew doesn't break up too much.

When the caponata is ready, set it aside to chill somewhat while you prepare the bruschetta. Heat a griddle pan, sprinkle the bread with olive oil, and griddle until both sides are toasted and gently charred, then rub with a garlic clove and season. Serve the warm caponata with bruschetta on the side, garnished with pine nuts and basil leaves.

Mediterranean fig & mozzarella salad

Ingredients

- 1 tablespoon fig jam or relish
- 200g fine green bean, trimmed
- 3 tablespoon balsamic vinegar

- 3 tablespoon extra-virgin olive oil
- 50g hazelnut, toasted and chopped
- small handful basil leaves, torn
- 6 small figs, quartered
- 1 shallot, thinly sliced x ball mozzarella, drained and ripped into chunks

Method

In a large pot, blanch the beans for 2-3 minutes in salted water. Drain on paper towels after rinsing with cold water. Serve on a serving platter. On top, there are hazelnuts, basil, mozzarella, figs, and shallots.

In a small bowl with a tight-fitting lid, combine the vinegar, fig jam, olive oil, and spices. Give it a thorough shake right before serving and pour it over the salad.

Pancetta-wrapped fish with lemony potatoes

Ingredients

- 1 lemon
- 100g green bean small handful black kalamata
- 2 chunky pollock fillets
- 2 tablespoon olive oil

- 300g new potato
- olives zest and juice

Method

Preheat the oven to 200 degrees Celsius. Boil the potatoes for 10 minutes, or until done, in a kettle of water. Add the beans in the last 2 minutes of cooking. Drain the potatoes completely before cutting them in half. In a large baking dish, combine the tomatoes, olives, lemon zest, and oil. Season with salt and pepper to taste.

Salt and pepper the fish before wrapping it in pancetta or bacon. Put the potatoes on top of that. Serve with a squeeze of lemon juice and a sprinkling of tarragon after baking for 10 minutes, or until cooked through.

Polenta, roasted vegetables & peppered Parmesan crisps

Ingredients

- ½ teaspoon salt
- 1 small butternut squash
- 2 teaspoon freshly picked thyme leaf
- 200g fine polenta

- 3 raw beetroot
- 50g butter
- 60g grated cheese
- small red onion
- tablespoon olive oil
- juice of ½ lemon

Method

Preheat the oven to 200°C for the crisps. Sprinkle a liberal teaspoon of black pepper over the grated Parmesan and spread equally on a baking tray fitted with silicone sheets or lightly oiled greaseproof paper.

Preheat the oven to 350 degrees Fahrenheit and bake for 5 minutes, or until golden but not browned. Allow the mixture to chill for five minutes before breaking it up with your fingertips into crisp pieces.

Preheat the oven to 220 degrees Fahrenheit. Season the squash and beetroot chunks with salt and pepper, then roast in a roasting pan with lemon juice and oil for 20 minutes. Bake for another 20 minutes after adding the onion wedges.

Meanwhile, in a large pot, bring a liter of water, salt, and half the butter to a simmer, then slowly pour in the polenta while continually stirring. Cook for an additional 30 minutes on low heat, stirring frequently to avoid sticking.

At this time, the polenta should be thickened but still soft. Add a cup of water if it starts to dry out too much. Add the remaining butter, Taleggio, parmesan, and a pinch of white pepper when the pasta is done.

Spread the polenta on a board or plates, then top with the vegetables and any roasting juices, followed by the rocket and thyme.

Spinach with chili & lemon crumbs

Ingredients

- 100g fresh breadcrumb
- 1 lemon
- 2 garlic cloves, crushed
- 25g butter
- 500g spinach
- 1 red chili, finely chopped

Method

Melt the butter in a large frying pan, then add the breadcrumbs, chile, zest, and garlic when it begins to boil.

Cook for about 10 minutes, or until golden brown and crisp. After taking it from the pan and sprinkling it with salt and pepper, set it aside.

Stir in the spinach to wilt it in the pan. Season to taste with salt and pepper, then sprinkle with crispy crumbs.

Mediterranean chicken traybake

Ingredients

- 1 red onion, cut into wedges
- 1 red pepper, deseeded and cut into chunks
- 150g pack full-fat garlic & herb soft cheese
- 2 teaspoon olive oil
- 200g pack cherry tomatoes
- 4 skin-on chicken breasts
- handful black olives

Method

Preheat the oven to 200 degrees Celsius. In a large baking dish, combine the peppers and onion with half of the oil. Bake for 10 minutes on the upper level of the oven.

In the meantime, make a pocket between the skin and the flesh of each chicken breast, but don't remove the skin completely. In the tray with the tomatoes and olives, push equal amounts of cheese under the skin, smooth it back down, coat it with the remaining oil, season it, and place it there. Return the chicken to the oven for a final 25-30 minutes, or until golden brown and well cooked.

Serve with baked potatoes if preferred.

Mussels with tomatoes & chili

Ingredients

- 1 garlic clove, finely chopped
- 1 red or green chili, deseeded and finely chopped small glass dry white wine
- 1 shallot, finely chopped
- 1 teaspoon tomato paste pinch of sugar
- 1kg cleaned mussels good handful basil leaves

- 2 ripe tomatoes

- 2 tablespoon olive oil

Method

In a heatproof bowl, place the tomatoes. Cover with boiling water and let aside for 3 minutes before draining and peeling. Using a teaspoon, scrape out and discard the seeds from the tomatoes. Chop the tomato flesh coarsely.

In a big pan with a tight-fitting lid, heat the oil. Gently sauté the garlic, shallot, and chile for 2-3 minutes, or until softened. Pour in the wine, then add the tomatoes, paste, and sugar, seasoning with salt and pepper to taste. Cook for 2 minutes after stirring thoroughly.

Stir in the mussels until they are thoroughly mixed. Cover closely and steam for 3-4 minutes, until the shells have opened, shaking the pan halfway through.

Any leftover shells should be discarded, and the mussels should be divided between two bowls and garnished with basil leaves. Half-fill a big bowl with empty shells.

Roasted peppers with tomatoes & anchovies

Ingredients

- 2 garlic cloves, thinly sliced
- 2 rosemary sprigs
- 2 tablespoon olive oil
- 4 red peppers, halved and deseeded
- 50g can anchovy in oil, drained
- 8 smallish tomatoes, halved

Method

Preheat the oven to 160 degrees Celsius. Place the peppers cut-side up in a large baking dish and mix with a little of the anchovy can's oil. Cook until the potatoes are tender but not mushy, about 40 minutes.

Cut eight anchovies in half lengthwise. In the hollows of each pepper, place two tomato halves, several garlic slices, a few rosemary sprigs, and two anchovy pieces..

Drizzle the olive oil on top and bake for another 30 minutes, or until the tomatoes are tender and the peppers are overflowing with delicious juice. Allow to cool completely before serving warm or at room temperature..

Easy stuffed peppers

Ingredients

- 2 pouches cooked tomato rice
- 2 tablespoon pesto
- 200g goat's cheese, sliced
- 4 red peppers

Method

Cut the tops off four red peppers with a tiny knife and scrape out the seeds. Cut-side up on a plate, microwave the peppers for 5 minutes on High, or until wilted and softened.

While the peppers are cooking, combine the two cooked tomato rice, 2 tablespoons pesto, a handful of pitted black olives, and 140g sliced goat's cheese in a mixing bowl.Half of the peppers should be filled with goat cheese mixture, rice, pesto, and olives, and the remaining 60g sliced goat's cheese should be on top. Cook for an additional ten minutes.

Crunchy baked mussels

Ingredients

- 1 lemon
- 100g garlic and parsley butter
- 1kg mussel in their shells
- 50g toasted breadcrumb

Method

Scrub the mussels to remove any beards that have formed. Rinse several times in cold water before discarding any that are open and do not close when tapped against the side of the sink.

Remove the mussels from their shells and place them in a large pot with some water. Bring to a boil, then cover and shake the pan occasionally for about 2 minutes, or until the mussels open. Drain thoroughly and discard any that are still closed. Heat the grill to a high setting.

In a mixing dish, combine the crumbs and zest. Remove one side of each mussel's shell, then brush each one with a small bit of butter. Place on a baking tray and top with crumbs. 4 minutes on the grill, or until crisp.

Aïoli

Ingredients

- 1 tablespoon Dijon mustard
- 2 egg yolks
- 3 garlic cloves, crushed
- 300ml olive oil
- small pinch saffron strands

Method

1 tablespoon boiling water + 1 tablespoon saffron.

In a food processor or blender, combine the egg yolk, garlic, and mustard. To make a thick mayonnaise-style sauce, blitz the ingredients into a paste and slowly drizzle in the olive oil. Add the lemon, saffron, and saffron water after everything has come together, and season to taste.

The aoli will keep in the fridge for up to 2 days if kept covered.

Watermelon & feta salad with crispbread

Ingredients

- olive oil

- balsamic vinegar, to serve

- 200g block feta cheese, cubed large handful black olives handful flat-leaf parsley and mint leaves, roughly chopped

- 1 red onion, finely sliced into rings

- ½ a watermelon

For the crispbread

- a mix of fennel seed, sesame seeds, and poppy seeds for scattering

- 1 tablespoon olive oil, plus a little extra for drizzling plain flour, for dusting

- 1 egg white, beaten

- ½ 500g pack white bread mix

Method

Prepare the bread according to the package guidelines using 1 tablespoon olive oil. Allow to rise in a warm place for 1 hour, or until it has doubled in size. Preheat oven to 220 degrees Fahrenheit. Cut the bread into 6 pieces after returning it to its original position.

On a floured surface, roll out the as thinly as possible, then transfer to baking trays.

After brushing with the egg white, scatter the mixed seeds. Bake for 15 minutes, or until crisp and brown; a little bubbling is even better. There's a chance you'll have to do this in bunches. They can be made in advance and kept in an airtight container. Toss the melon with the feta cheese and serve.

Sprinkle the onions and herbs over top, then drizzle with balsamic vinegar and olive oil.

Crispy squid with caponata

Ingredients

- 800g cleaned squid tubes
- 150g plain flour
- 1 tablespoon cayenne pepper
- sunflower oil , for frying

For the caponata

- 4 tablespoon extra-virgin olive oil
- 30g caper
- 3 garlic cloves , crushed
- 3 celery sticks, sliced
- 250g cherry tomatoes
- 1 large aubergine
- 1 onion , chopped
- 1 tablespoon balsamic vinegar
- 1 teaspoon caster sugar
- 150g green olive , stoned

Method

Place the squid flat on a board to cook it. Cut along one side with a long, thin knife inserted into the aperture. Scrape away any residual membrane by opening it up to a flat sheet.

Lightly score the flesh in a diamond pattern with the point of the knife, being careful not to cut through the squid entirely. Squid should be cut into large triangles before being floured and fried.

To make the caponata, chop the aubergine into uniform dice: 1cm thick lengthwise slice, then cut long strips of the same size, then chop into squares.

In a large sauté pan, heat half of the oil. Fry the onions for 4 minutes, or until they begin to soften, then add the aubergine and cook for another 10 minutes, or until golden and tender. Place in a colander over a basin to drain.

Return any remaining oil from the bowl to the pan and top it over with a splash of new oil. Combine the celery, tomatoes, and smashed garlic in a pan. Sprinkle the sugar on top, then add the vinegar and heat for 3-4 minutes, or until the tomatoes begin to release juice.

Return the aubergine and onion to the pot, along with the celery. Stir in the olives, capers, and basil until everything is well combined. Cook for 5 minutes, or until the sauce has reached a simmer, then season to taste. Remove from the heat, drizzle with the remaining oil, and set aside.

Transfer the squid to a big mixing bowl just before cooking. Toss the squid with the flour and cayenne pepper, then season with salt and pepper. Return the squid to the sieve and shake off any remaining flour.

Fill a big frying pan halfway with sunflower oil, about 1cm deep. When a pinch of flour is sprinkled into the oil, it sizzles. Fry the squid in batches for 3 minutes. When the squid is done, transfer it to a platter lined with kitchen paper using tongs. You're now ready to start serving.

Place the caponata in the middle of a medium dinner plate inside a 10cm wide metal ring. Lightly press down on the caponata with the back of the spoon to level the top of the mound. Carefully peel the ring away from the caponata tower, keeping it round. Serve immediately after leaning five or six pieces of squid around the caponata like petals on a flower.

Spiced baked figs with ginger mascarpone

Ingredients

- shortbread fingers, to serve
- For the ginger mascarpone
- 8 figs , halved

- 2 teaspoon ground cinnamon
- ½ a 250g tub mascarpone
- 1 ball stem ginger , very finely chopped
- 1 tablespoon ginger syrup from the jar
- 2 tablespoon brown sugar
- 2 tablespoon butter
- 2 tablespoon clear honey
- 2 tablespoon orange juice

Method

Preheat the oven to 200 degrees Fahrenheit. Place the figs in an ovenproof roasting dish, drizzle with honey, and dot with butter. Sprinkle the sugar and cinnamon on top, then pour in the orange juice and gently combine. Roast for 20 minutes with the star anise nestled among the figs.

When ready to serve, fold the mascarpone into the ginger and syrup. 4 fig halves drizzled with syrup, a dollop of mascarpone, and some shortbread fingers on a plate

Mediterranean scones

Ingredients

- 1 egg , beaten, to glaze
- 1 tablespoon baking powder
- 1 tablespoon olive oil
- 10 black olives , pitted and halved
- 100g feta cheese , cubed
- 300ml full fat milk
- 350g self-rising flour
- 50g butter , cut in pieces
- 8 halves Italian sundried tomatoes, coarsely chopped
- ¼ teaspoon salt

Method

Preheat the oven to 220°C with the door ajar. Using butter, grease a large baking sheet.

Combine the flour, salt and baking powder in a large mixing bowl. Add the tomatoes, cheese, and olives after rubbing the butter and oil together.

Make a well in the center, pour in the milk, and stir with a knife in a cutting motion until the dough becomes a soft,'stickyish' consistency. Don't handle the dough too much.

Flour your hands and work surface well, then roll out the dough into a 3-4cm thick round. Cut into eight wedges and arrange on a baking sheet far apart. Brush with beaten egg and bake for 20 minutes, or until risen, golden, and springy.

To keep them soft, place them on a wire rack and cover with a clean tea towel. Warm and buttered is the finest way to serve these. In an airtight container, it will last for 3 days.

Mediterranean turkey-stuffed peppers

Ingredients

- ½ small onion, chopped
- 1 ½ tablespoon olive oil, plus an extra drizzle
- 1 chicken stock cube
- 1 garlic clove, grated
- 1 tablespoon tomato purée
- 1 teaspoon ground cumin
- 150g green vegetables to serve
- 2 red peppers
- 240g lean turkey breast mince

- 3-4 mushrooms, sliced
- 400g can chopped tomatoes
- 60g mozzarella, grated
- handful fresh oregano leaves

Method

Heat oven to 190C. Halve the peppers lengthways, then remove the seeds and core but keep the stems on. Season the peppers with a drizzle of olive oil and salt & pepper to taste. Roast for 15 minutes on a baking tray.

Meanwhile, in a big pan over medium heat, heat 1 tablespoon olive oil. Cook for 3 minutes, stirring to break up the chunks, before transferring to a platter.

Clean your pan and heat the remaining oil over medium-high heat. Stir in the onion and garlic for 3 minutes, then add the cumin and mushrooms and simmer for another 3 minutes.

Return the mince to the pan and stir in the tomato purée and chopped tomatoes. Cook for 3 minutes after adding the stock cube, then season with oregano. Remove the peppers from the oven and stuff them as full as you can with the mince. Return to the oven for another 10-15 minutes, or until the cheese begins to become brown.

Carefully transfer the peppers to a platter and serve with a heaping of blanched, boiled, or steamed greens.

Speedy Mediterranean gnocchi

Ingredients

- 2 tablespoon red pesto
- 200g chargrilled vegetables
- 400g gnocchi
- handful of basil leaves
- parmesan

Method

Bring a big pot of salted water to a boil. Cook for 2 minutes, or until the gnocchi rises to the surface, then drain and return to the pan with a splash of the reserved cooking water.

Add the chargrilled vegetables, red pesto, and basil leaves, chopped into bits if they're large.

Mediterranean fig & mozzarella salad

Ingredients

- 1 shallot
- 1 tablespoon fig jam
- 200g fine green bean , trimmed
- small handful basil leaves, torn
- 6 small figs
- 50g hazelnut
- 3 tablespoon extra-virgin olive oil
- 3 tablespoon balsamic vinegar

Method

Parboil the beans in salted water for 3 minutes. After rinsing with cold water, drain on paper towels. Place on a serving plate to serve. hazelnuts, Basil, shallots, figs, mozzarella are sprinkled on top.

Combine the olive oil, vinegar, fig jam, and spices in a small bowl with a tight-fitting cover. Just before serving, give it a good shake and pour it over the salad.

Turkey taco lettuce boat

Ingredients

- 1 cup salsa chipotle
- 1 medium peeled and chopped onion 2 large peeled and diced carrots
- 1 peeled, pitted, and sliced medium avocado
- 1 pound turkey ground
- 1 tablespoon paprika
- 1 teaspoon cumin
- 1 tsp cayenne pepper
- 12 romaine lettuce leaves
- 2 garlic cloves, minced
- 2 medium celery stalks, peeled and diced
- a half teaspoon of salt
- a quarter teaspoon of black pepper
- avocado oil, 1 tbsp

Press the Sauté button after adding the oil. Before adding the onion, carrots, celery, and garlic, let the oil heat for 1 minute. Cook for 5 minutes, or until the vegetables are softened.

Cook for another 3 minutes, or until the turkey is golden brown.

Add the salsa, chili powder, paprika, cumin, salt, and pepper to taste. Press the Cancel button to end the session. Put the lid back on.

By clicking the Manual or Pressure Cook button, you can reduce the cooking time to 15 minutes.

When the timer beeps, quickly release pressure until the float valve drops.

Serve taco meat with lettuce and avocado slices on the side.

Lemon ginger broccoli and carrots

- 1 garlic clove, peeled and minced
- 1 inch peeled and finely sliced fresh ginger
- 1 quart of water
- 1/2 a huge lemon's juice
- 2 big peeled and thinly sliced carrots
- 2 broccoli heads cut into big florets with stems removed

- avocado oil, 1 tbsp

- kosher salt (1/2 teaspoon)

Press the Sauté button after adding the oil. Before adding the onion, carrots, celery, and garlic, let the oil heat for 1 minute. Cook for 5 minutes, or until the vegetables are softened.

Cook for another 3 minutes, or until the turkey is golden brown.

Add the salsa, chili powder, paprika, cumin, salt, and pepper to taste. Press the Cancel button to end the session. Put the lid back on.

By clicking the Manual or Pressure Cook button, you can reduce the cooking time to 15 minutes.

When the timer beeps, quickly release pressure until the float valve drops.

Serve taco meat with lettuce and avocado slices on the side.

Serve

Spinach and eggs scrambled with raspberry

- 1 tblsp. canola seed oil

- 2 big, lightly beaten eggs

- 1 tsp. kosher salt

- a pinch of black pepper

- 1 toasted whole-grain bread slice

- 12 cup raspberries, fresh

- 12 cup (1 1/2 ounces) baby spinach

In a small nonstick skillet, heat the oil over medium-high heat. Cook, tossing frequently, until the spinach has wilted, about 1 to 2 minutes. Place the spinach on a serving platter.

Clean the pan, place it over medium heat, and crack the eggs into it. Cook, stirring once or twice to ensure equal cooking, for 1 to 2 minutes, or until just set. Add the spinach, salt, and pepper to taste. With toast and strawberries, serve the scramble.

Egg salad avocado toast

- 1 hard-boiled egg, chopped

- 1 teaspoon of salt

- 1 whole-wheat bread piece

- 12 tbsp lemon juice

- 12 tbsp. hot sauce

- 14 oz. avocado
- celery, 1 tbsp

In a small bowl, mash the avocado with the lemon juice, celery, lemon juice, spicy sauce, and salt. Add the hard-boiled egg to the mix. Spread on a piece of toast.

Smoked salmon and cream cheese omelette

- 1 tablespoon of butter
- 1 tablespoon red onion, finely chopped
- 1 tablespoon softened cream cheese or crumbled feta
- 1 teaspoon of salt
- 1 tsp. reduced-fat milk or 1 tsp. water
- 1/8 teaspoon ground pepper, with a little more for decoration
- 12 tablespoons fresh dill chopped, plus more for garnish
- 2 eggs, big
- 2 tbsp. smoked salmon, chopped

Whisk together the eggs, milk (or water), pepper, and salt in a small bowl.

Melt butter in a small nonstick skillet over medium-low heat, swirling the pan to coat the bottom completely. After adding the egg mixture, cook for 1 minute without stirring. Salmon, cheddar, onion, and dill should be put on half of the eggs. 1 minute of preparation With a flexible spatula, lift the bare side of the pan to allow raw egg from the middle to flow below; the pan may need to be tilted slightly. Lift in several locations until there is almost no raw egg remaining on top.

Cook for 1 minute after flipping the omelet over the filling and folding it in half. Carefully flip the omelet. Flip the omelet carefully and cook for another minute. Serve right away with more dill and pepper, if desired.

Glowing spiced lentil soup

- Freshly ground black pepper, to taste

- 3/4 cup uncooked red lentils, rinsed and drained

- 3 1/2 cups low-sodium vegetable broth

- 2 teaspoons ground turmeric

- 2 teaspoons fresh lime juice, or more to taste

- 2 large garlic cloves, minced

- 2 cups (280 grams) diced onion (1 medium/large)

- 1/4 teaspoon ground cardamom

- 1/2 teaspoon fine sea salt, or to taste

- 1/2 teaspoon cinnamon

- 1 1/2 teaspoons ground cumin

- 1 1/2 tablespoons (22.5 mL) extra-virgin olive oil

- 1 (5-ounce/140-gram) package baby spinach

- 1 (14-ounce/398 mL) can full-fat coconut milk*

- 1 (14-ounce/398 mL) can diced tomatoes, with juices

- Red pepper flakes to taste

In a large pot, combine the oil, onion, and garlic. Add a pinch of salt, stir, and simmer over medium heat for 4 to 5 minutes, or until the onion softens.

In a large mixing basin, combine the turmeric, cumin, cinnamon, and cardamom. Cook for another minute or so, until the mixture is fragrant.

Toss in the diced tomatoes (with juices), coconut milk (entire can), red lentils, broth, and season to taste with salt and pepper. Taste and season with cayenne or red pepper flakes, if desired. To blend, combine all of the ingredients in a mixing bowl. Bring the mixture to a low boil by increasing the heat to high.

Reduce the heat to medium-high and continue to cook, uncovered, for about 18 minutes, or until the lentils are frothy and soft.

Remove the pan from the heat and whisk in the spinach until it has wilted. To taste, add the lime juice. If desired, season with extra salt and pepper. Serve with toasted bread and lime wedges, ladled into bowls.

Mediterranean tuna salad

- Sundried tomatoes, chopped

- Red Wine Vinaigrette

- Pinch of fine sea salt

- Pinch of black pepper

- Pinch of black pepper

- Pinch fine salt

- 2 teaspoons capers

- 2 tbsp red wine vinegar

- 2 tablespoons olive oil

- 2 cans Genova Seafood Yellowfin Tuna or Albacore Tuna, drained

- 1/3 cup parsley, finely chopped

- 1/2 red onion, diced

- 1/2 cup pepperocini, diced

- 1/2 avocado, diced

- 1 teaspoon lemon juice

- 1 teaspoon dried parsley

- 1 teaspoon dried oregano

- 1 cup roasted red peppers, chopped

- 1 cucumber, chopped

Combine the oil, onion, and garlic in a big pot. Add a pinch of salt, stir, and cook for 4 to 5 minutes over medium heat, or until the onion softens.

Combine the turmeric, cumin, cinnamon, and cardamom in a large mixing bowl. Cook for a minute or two more, until the combination is aromatic.

Toss in the diced tomatoes (with juices), coconut milk (entire can), red lentils, and broth, seasoning to taste. If desired, add cayenne or red pepper flakes to taste. In a mixing dish, add all of the ingredients to blend. Increase the heat to high and bring the mixture to a low boil.

Reduce the heat to medium-high and simmer for another 18 minutes, uncovered, or until the lentils are foamy and soft.

Remove the pan from the heat and add the spinach, whisking constantly until the spinach has wilted. Add the lime juice to taste. Season with more salt and pepper if required.

Sun dried tomato red lentil pasta

Ingredients

- kosher salt and pepper

- grated parmesan, nutritional yeast, toasted pine nuts and or seeds, for topping

- 6 cloves garlic, minced or grated

- 2 teaspoons ground turmeric

- 2 large handfuls baby spinach or kale

- 1/4 cup extra virgin olive oil

- 1/2 cup oil packed sun-dried tomatoes, oil

- 1 tablespoon dried oregano

- 1 tablespoon dried basil

- 1 tablespoon apple cider vinegar

- 1 sweet onion, chopped

- 1 (8 ounce) box red lentil pasta or other short cut pasta

- 1 (28 ounce) can fire roasted tomatoes

In a large pot over medium heat, heat the olive oil. When the oil begins to shimmer, add the onion and simmer for 5-10 minutes, or until tender and caramelized. Garlic, basil, oregano, turmeric, salt, and pepper are added. Cook for 1 minute, or until the mixture is aromatic. Slowly pour in the tomatoes and their juices, smashing the tomatoes with the back of a wooden spoon as you go. Toss in the sun-dried tomatoes and balsamic vinegar. Simmer for 10-15 minutes, or until the sauce has somewhat reduced. You can purée the sauce in a blender if desired.

Cook for another five minutes after adding the spinach.

Meanwhile, bring a large pot of salted water to a boil and cook the pasta until al dente, as directed on the package. Drain.

Toss the pasta with a liberal quantity of sauce in each bowl. Cheese, nuts, and herbs can be added as desired.

Honey mustard pork with spinach and smashed white beans
Ingredients

- 3 tablespoons honey

- 3 tablespoons extra-virgin olive oil, divided

- 2 tablespoons whole-grain mustard

- 2 cloves garlic, minced

- 2 (15 ounce) cans low-sodium cannellini beans, rinsed

- 1 ½ teaspoons chopped fresh sage

- 1 ¼ pounds pork tenderloin, trimmed

- 1 pound mature spinach, chopped

- ¾ cup low-sodium chicken broth, divided

- ½ teaspoon salt, divided

- ½ teaspoon ground pepper

- ¼ teaspoon crushed red pepper

Preheat the oven to 425 degrees Fahrenheit.

Pork should be seasoned with 1/4 teaspoon salt and pepper. In a large ovenproof skillet, heat 1 tablespoon oil over medium-high heat. Cook, rotating frequently, until the pork is browned on all sides, 3 to 5 minutes total. Preheat the oven to 350°F. For about 15 minutes, roast until an instant-read thermometer placed in the center reads 145 degrees F.

Meanwhile, in a big pot over medium-high heat, heat 1 tablespoon oil. Cook, stirring constantly, for 2 to 3 minutes, until spinach is wilted. Place in a basin and cover to stay warm.

In the same saucepan, heat the remaining 1 tablespoon oil over medium heat. Cook for 30 seconds after adding the garlic, sage, and crushed red pepper. Combine the beans, 1/2 cup broth, and the remaining 1/8 teaspoon salt in a large mixing bowl. Using a potato masher, mash the potatoes until they are virtually smooth. Reduce heat to low and simmer, stirring frequently, until well heated, about 5 minutes. Remove the pan from the heat and cover it.

Allow the pork to rest for 5 minutes on a clean chopping board. In a separate pan, combine the honey, mustard, and the remaining 1/4 cup broth. Over medium-high heat, bring to a boil, scraping up any browned bits. Reduce heat to low and cook for 1 to 2 minutes, or until slightly thickened.

Pork should be sliced. Serve with mashed beans, spinach, and sauce on the side.

Scallion-ginger beef and broccoli

Ingredients

- ¼ cup low-sodium chicken broth

- ⅓ cup reduced-sodium tamari or soy sauce

- ½ cup sliced scallions, plus more for garnish

- 1 pound sirloin steak, thinly sliced

- 1 tablespoon finely grated ginger

- 1 teaspoon finely grated garlic

- 2 cups cooked brown rice

- 2 tablespoons brown sugar

- 2 tablespoons cornstarch, divided

- 3 tablespoons peanut or canola oil, divided

- 6 cups broccoli florets

- Crushed red pepper for garnish

In a small bowl, combine the brown sugar, tamari (or soy sauce), broth, and 1 tablespoon cornstarch. Toss the steak with the last tablespoon of cornstarch.

In a large flat-bottom wok or cast-iron skillet, heat 2 tablespoons oil over medium-high heat. Cook, tossing once, until the meat is browned, about 4 minutes. Place on a clean platter. Cook, stirring occasionally, until slightly soft, with the remaining 1 tablespoon oil and broccoli. Cook, stirring constantly, until the scallions, ginger, and garlic are fragrant, about 30 seconds. Return the tamari mixture to the pan, along with the meat, and heat for 1 minute, or until the sauce thickens.

- 4 cups reduced-sodium vegetable broth

- 2 tablespoons extra-virgin olive oil

- 2 cups cauliflower florets

- 1 ½ teaspoons lime juice

- 1 ¼ cups well-shaken light coconut milk, divided

- 1 teaspoon ground cumin

- 1 teaspoon ground coriander

- 1 tablespoon minced fresh ginger

- 1 small serrano pepper, seeded and chopped

- 1 medium yellow onion, chopped

- 1 medium butternut squash

- ¾ teaspoon toasted fennel seeds, divided

- ½ teaspoon salt

- ½ teaspoon ground turmeric

In a large Dutch oven or heavy stockpot, heat the oil over medium heat. Cook, stirring frequently, for about 7 minutes, or until the onion is transparent. Cook, stirring frequently, until the serrano and ginger are aromatic, about 1 minute.

Reduce the heat to low and stir in the coriander, cumin, turmeric, and 1/4 teaspoon fennel seeds. Cook, stirring constantly, for 1 minute, or until aromatic. Combine the cauliflower and broth in a mixing bowl. Bring to a boil over medium-high heat; lower to medium-low heat and cook, stirring periodically, for 25 to 30 minutes, or until the squash is fork-tender.

Transfer the squash mixture to a blender in two batches. Remove the center piece from the blender and secure the lid to allow steam to escape. Cover the opening with a clean cloth. Process for 1 minute, or until smooth.Toss the mixture back into the pot.

1 cup coconut milk, stirred into the soup Over medium-low heat, bring to a slow simmer. Combine the lime juice and salt in a mixing bowl. Remove the pan from the heat.

Pour the soup into four bowls. 1 tablespoon coconut milk and a sprinkling of fennel seeds on top of each.

Conclusion

Though there is no one-size-fits-all Mediterranean diet, it is generally high in healthful plant foods and low in animal foods, with a focus on fish and shellfish.

It has been linked to a variety of health advantages, including helping to regulate blood sugar levels, increase heart health, and improve cognitive function, among others.

The best part is that you may customize the Mediterranean diet to suit your needs. If you don't care for salmon or sardines but enjoy whole wheat pasta and olive oil, start putting together great Mediterranean-inspired meals with things you enjoy.